I0413545

Of GOLD and BITCOINS

How We Arrived At Crypto Currency And How To Get A Piece Of The Action!

**ISBN-13: 978-1497533004**

**ISBN-10: 1497533007**

Concept by Russell Webster

Written by

VIBENODE

Edited by Tony Cowger

Thanks to Mark Pope.

Published by Snafu

All contact-

russell@snafu.co

# Introduction

We live in abstract times! We are buying and selling in nothing more than lies and promises of commodities that have long since surpassed the actual amount of the commodities themselves. As the planet stands today we are at a tipping point, unlike any we have ever known before. Due to our technology accelerating at a rate which is making science fiction a reality and the world unified through the internet, the need for a revolutionary method in which to trade is upon us!

We are about to venture into the brave unknown with regards to the way in which we store our wealth and trade our good and services. Hopefully, we will come out together on the other side as a new, enlightened breed of mankind.

This book is by no means a definitive guide, nor is it supposed to be. There is so much resource material out there if you look carefully enough and open your eyes to just how wrong our current monetary system is, and has been for centuries. Each section has enough content available for a book in its own right. The aim with this book/book/ebooks merely trying to break this all down into a format where you can draw down the information you need in compressed form, along with some interesting facts that go hand in hand with the pertinent information. After reading, if you wish, you can take action to protect the interests of yourself as well as your friends and families as we move forward into the new age.

Yesterday is history,
Tomorrows a mystery,
Today is a gift,
Enjoy your present!          VibeNode

# Contents

# 1. Animal To Man

Since the birth of modern mankind there has always existed the need to trade goods and services between individuals. The term modern mankind, as it is used here, is not in reference to the last 100 years, or even the last 1000. It is more like 10,000 years, before which we were closer to animals than modern humans. Technology has advanced so fast in the last few decades that even 20 years ago seems primitive now. Back then, mobile phones were brick sized car phones, hardly anybody owned a home PC, and the internet was still in its infancy. When you get a sense of scale that the oldest Homo Sapiens date back over 150,000 years, and we were even more primitive forms of man for millions of years before this, 10,000 years suddenly doesn't seem like such a long time. If you were to represent the age of the Earth, which is 4.6 Billion years, as 4.6 minutes, mankind doesn't even take up a single second on that timescale.

As we have evolved to where we are today, we have developed many other needs with regards to comfort and personal happiness. Our basic needs are food, water, and shelter. Whatever your interests are, if you strip all those away we are still left with the same fundamental survival needs we have always had. We all need to eat, we all need water and we all need shelter.

We used to take care of all these needs ourselves, much like any other animal does. Primitive man would have found shelter, usually typified by a cave. They would know where the supplies of fresh running water would be. Finally, they would forage and hunt, stereotypically with a sharp piece of flint lashed to a stick. Herbs, roots, fruit and vegetables would be foraged for food, and possibly very early types of medicine. Game like deer and rabbits, would be hunted, again for food; but the hide would be used to create clothing or even primitive footwear. Each man would most likely do all these things many times a day to ensure continued survival.

Going far enough back many say we would only have foraged for food, we are not and have never been designed to be carnivores, though we have successfully evolved into omnivores and can now eat meat in our diets. Take our ape cousins for example, many of which have very powerful bodies which could be used to kill another animal very successfully if required, but the majority of them are more than content with foraging and can survive on this alone. Further evidence also compounds this, such as our physical attributes, mainly focussed on how we eat and digest our food.

Let's look at the attributes of a carnivore. A carnivore has a very large mouth to head ratio, allowing large quantities of meat to be eaten quickly. The teeth of a meat eating creature are all sharp and pointed, designed to shear off bits of flesh and swallow them whole. Their jaws also allow them little movement other than the opening and closing of the mouth. Their nails are a similar shape as the teeth to further aid the rendering of flesh. A carnivore has little or no digestive enzymes in their saliva, as the whole digestive process is performed in the stomach, and the length of their digestive tracts are between 4 and 6 times their body length. Their stomach size is a large percentage of their digestive tracts, as much as 70%, and has a very low pH giving a highly acidic level of pH 1 or less.

For herbivores the mouth to head ratio is very small. Teeth are flat to allow the grinding down of plants and the jaw allows movement in many directions to aid this, back to front and side to side. The nails are flat as they are not required to tear flesh or aid them with a kill. A herbivore has digestive enzymes in their saliva so the food is already being broken down before it reaches the stomach, or in some cases, stomachs. The length of the digestive tract is many times their body length, as much as 12 times. Their percentage of stomach size to digestive tract is also considerably lower, less than 30%, as much of the absorption of nutrients happens in the intestines. The pH of the stomach is also higher, and so less acidic, at around pH 4.

Let's apply this to man today. Our mouth to head ratio is very small. Our teeth and nails are not sharp or pointed, even our front teeth designed to shear are spade shaped and not ending in a point, our jaws are also omnidirectional. We all know digestion begins in our mouth as our saliva does contain digestive enzymes, which, apart from choking, is why we are encouraged to thoroughly chew our food. Our digestive tracks are around 10 times our body length, very close to a herbivores, and share a very similar percentage stomach capacity and pH level.

When looking at creatures that are designed to be omnivores, their qualities are almost identical to a carnivore in every way. So, in many respects, although we can eat meat, physiologically we are still designed to be herbivores even now.

How is this relevant? It displays clearly our amazing ability to adapt to survive, to see a challenge presented and find a solution. The most logical reason why we could have started eating meat is simply due to opportunity. Put in a situation where there was not enough food to forage, killing and eating another animal would most likely have been the only option. If it's a choice between starving and not, eating meat is definitely logical.

Whatever the original diet, very few places on the planet had the required sustenance to provide a permanent solution for hunter/gatherer man, so they re-located frequently. Once an area had been exhausted for nutrition, they would move on until they found a new area with all the requirements and settle here for a period, until the same happened again and they were ready to move on once more. Vegetation takes time to grow back and they may have operated a cycle between locations on an annual basis or longer.

During this period, communities of man were very small, more of a pack that we associate with wolves and dogs. This is generally thought of to be a group of adults between 10 -20 and however many offspring came with them. There would have been a very definite pecking order, with a clear Alpha male and possibly female as well. Fighting between these tribes would also have been commonplace, and any invasion into their territory by a neighbouring or passing tribe would likely have been met with aggression and bloodshed as resources were defended.

As we well know, man's greatest asset is his brain, and his ability to communicate more efficiently than any other creature. As mankind continued to evolve and further improve his communication skills, he began to form communities, and these grew into larger and larger collectives. When this happened he realised that he could trade things he had for things he didn't and barter was born.

**This was the starting point, and very essence of all trading, which contributed massively to creating the first great civilizations of our species...**

## 2. Barter Trade

As man started to live in communities, it was discovered that some people possessed certain strengths others didn't. Some had the ability to hunt better than their neighbours, or an innate ability to tend to crops much better than others around them, giving a greater crop yield and quality of produce. Individuals started playing to their strengths, and specializing their skill-set to what would become the start of professions, many of which are here even today in some form or another.

Common items to trade were food, weapons, animal hides and salt. These were survival basics. Food for nutrition, weapons to hunt and defend themselves and their families, animal hides as clothing, and salt, a very highly valued commodity for its ability to preserve meat and fish.

To best explain barter, let's take this scenario: We have a hunter, a farmer and a fisherman. The fisherman would come to market with his daily catch, and while some of this he would need for

himself and his family, he would also need other goods, bread for instance. So, at the market the fisherman would approach the farmer. They would communicate what was deemed to be a fair deal and the fisherman would walk away with 2 loaves of bread for 1 fish, for example. He may also wish to trade some more of his catch for some venison, so the same thing happens with the hunter, and he trades 7 fish for a fresh side of deer. The fisherman simply does not have the time after a long day of fishing to grow wheat or hunt deer, and likewise the farmer and hunter have no time to fish after spending their days tending to crops or hunting in the woods, respectively.

It is this diversity that distinguishes us from other animals, alongside our ability to communicate what we can offer against something we don't have or can't acquire ourselves. This is the essence of all trade. I will offer you something you don't have or can't acquire, and in return you will offer me something I don't have or can't acquire. This ensures survival, and even comfort.

The best way of seeing bartering in action today is actually with children. All these hobbies that have emerged over the years, Pogs, Stickers, Trading Card Games, amongst others, are their commodities. Children very rarely have money to trade with, so they strike a deal with each other based on what they have against what they want. "I'll trade you these 2 rare cards and 7 common cards for those 3 rare cards." This is a common playground interaction. Much like bartering used to be, these discussions can often get quite heated as two young minds attempt to outsmart each other to get the most they possibly can out of the deal. Once both are satisfied, the exchange is made and they each walk away with their new commodities. If anything, this process is an essential part of paving their way to adulthood, teaching them from an early age how to communicate and interact with other.

Barter is not simply limited to trading goods for other goods. It could also be trading goods for a service, or even a service for a service. The hunter, while being an accomplished huntsman, may not be so adept at making traps, only setting them. The fisherman however, with a large part of his job making netting, would be just the right person for him to approach. The hunter provides the materials and the fisherman agrees to make some net traps for him, in return he desires some venison. The fisherman has provided nothing more than his time and skills in return for a commodity, a service for goods.

Expanding on the above example, the fisherman may not desire venison in return at all, but a service from the hunter. The hunter, while not adept at making netting would be competent at making spears. The fisherman in return may ask that if he provides the materials that the hunter makes some spears for him. At no point have any goods changed hands. They have simply traded each other for their time, a service for a service. Barter takes many forms and instead of trading each other in something with a set value, it is simply what you require based on what you are willing to give for it.

Barter is not without its flaws though. There were no standardized rates of exchange, and often the bartering process was lengthy until both parties were satisfied with what they were receiving, balanced against what they were giving in return. It also posed further problems. What if they simply didn't have a need for the goods you have to offer. What if the fisherman approached the hunter for some venison, but the hunter said he wanted bread not fish. The fisherman would then have to barter with the farmer for some bread, and then barter that bread against the venison. The farmer may realise the fisherman's high desire for the bread and charge him 1 fish per loaf instead of the usual fish for 2 loaves. Once the bread is acquired, the hunter may also realise the fisherman's desire for his venison, after having already traded his fish for bread; and offer him an even worse deal than usual, at the end of which the fisherman is very much out of pocket. Even worse than that, what if nobody desired fish? Then the fisherman is unable to trade with anyone. Barter trade's main flaw lies in it being a coincidence of wants/needs.

Even though today we have evolved the process into more effective manners in which to trade, bartering is by no means outdated, it just tends to remain between individuals, and even then usually between people we know. Say your friend's lawnmower has just broken beyond repair, and you have just treated yourself to a new one, with the old one still in good working order. Your friend is an electrician and you happen to want some wiring doing on your new extension. You have no further need for the old lawnmower so you offer it in exchange for some work to be done. He accepts your offer and you get your work done and get rid of the old lawnmower you no longer require. Both of you are up on the deal. The old lawnmower would have to be sold, stored or thrown; it has little further use to you with your shiny new one. In exchange you save having to pay someone to do the work you need done, and your electrician friend gets the lawnmower he needs for spending a day performing his trade. At no point is either person having to exchange money.

There are even cultures in isolated locations on the earth who still practice        barter        on        a        daily        basis.

It is estimated that 70% of the planets indigenous tribes still in existence are in Asia, and many have had little or no contact with the world outside their tribe or exposure to the technology we possess. How they must perceive us is something we really can't comprehend. In 2005, an aid helicopter that was flying over the Andaman and Nicobar Islands in southern Asia was actually shot at by bow and arrow. The only way we could possibly begin to understand this is by thinking of an alien spaceship appearing over a town or city.

It is also an interesting fact to note that during times of great financial hardship for communities or countries, such as the 1930's Great American Depression, people naturally revert back to bartering. When currency is scarce or becomes obsolete, we will always revert back to what we know, how to survive in any way possible. When faith is lost in a currency there is no longer any desire to obtain it, or receive it in a trade, and with good reason too. Who wants to give away their products, services and time in exchange for something that cannot be redeemed for another product or service at a later date? This risk is always present with our current monetary system, at any point something could destabilise a currency and cause a country to go into turmoil.

**For all its positives, barter trade had a very obvious downfall in that there were no standardised units of trade. It was only a matter of time before we developed a new manner in which to trade with each other...**

### 3. Gold & Silver

What exactly is gold and silver? Where does it come from? Why is it so valuable? These precious metals are formed when stars reach the end of their life and go supernova, spewing forth into space elements from all over the periodic table. All this space dust and debris will eventually be pulled together by gravity, usually during the formation of new planets. This puts the age of gold and silver

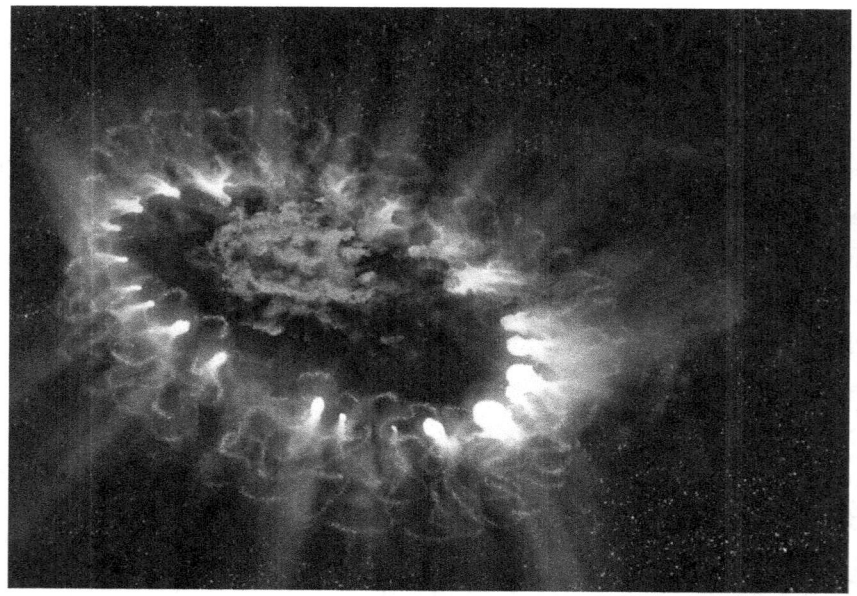

on our planet all the way back to the creation of the earth, 4.6 Billion years ago. They are in finite supply, and once we have mined or consumed them all there are no more to be obtained, on Earth,                                                                                                          anyway.

As established, without a standardized unit to use for trade, some people often get a bum deal or even find it impossible to trade at all. There were many things used as a form of money before we landed upon a real solution. The only prerequisite was that if you took payment for something in this money, you had the confidence that when you needed to buy something, it could be redeemed for the goods or services you required. One of the earliest trading mediums, maybe even the first, was conch shells.

As we again advance through our technology we discover these precious metals, and for a long time these offer us a reliable solution to the problem of a standardized method of trading. Precious metals are durable, non-perishable, and hold value in their own right. For these reasons they offered an ideal solution. Gold and silver, although not the only precious metals, became the two main mediums of exchange. Gold in particular became a highly effective manner in which to trade for a set price, so we will use this as our example. Instead of our tradesmen bartering with each other, they started trading goods for gold. Hence the expression, "worth its weight in gold" was born.

Using entirely fictitious measurements that are in no way designed to represent the actual trading values, let's say that a loaf of bread was 1 gram of gold, a fish was 2g, and a side of deer was 14 g of gold. As people buy fish from the fisherman, they pay him in weights of gold. With this gold he would then be able to take it to any other tradesman and give them his gold for their product or service. The farmer wants gold to trade with, as does the hunter, so now the fisherman will never be refused a trade as long as he can pay for it in gold.

When people think of the first metal we discovered many of us think about iron or copper, but gold was actually the very first metal that we stumbled upon, being found naturally in rivers and streams as well as in veins deep within the earth. It is also generally found in its natural state without the need to extract it from ores, as is the case with many other metals.

The earliest recorded use of gold goes back as far as 4600 B.C. to the Sumer civilization of Mesopotamia, where it was used for jewellery and headdresses. There have been tombs excavated dating from this period where the occupants were buried with these items.

Although not the first to use gold, the ancient Egyptians were the first to really expand on the use of gold as a trading medium. They were also the first civilization to mine for gold. As opposed to it being found naturally in rivers and streams the Egyptians actively sought it out in rock formations. It was thought of as the material or 'skin' of the gods. Many civilizations around this time worshipped the sun, and heralded it as a god. The Egyptians were no different. Gold in many ways represented a little bit of the sun on earth, and was revered due to this. In multi-god religions, or pantheons, the sun god was often thought of as the ruler of the other gods or at the least one of the upper echelon of deities. This was portrayed in ancient Egypt by the sun god, Ra. Given its yellow colour, its shiny properties, and how it catches and reflects light it is easy to see how this association was made.

What is little known is silver was initially just as valuable as gold in Egypt, but due to the 'Godlike' properties of gold the Egyptians soon became fanatical about it. Due to its status and association with the gods, only the most powerful men were originally allowed to own gold. As the Pharaohs were seen as manifestations of gods on earth they were initially the only ones to possess it, but the right to possess gold was eventually also granted to members of the priesthood and other members of the royal family. The goldsmiths of that era primarily used gold to create godlike likenesses into masks and other gilded objects that would be worn or displayed as a symbol of status. Eventually, gold would be granted as a privilege of the wealthy elite as well, and they used it to conduct trade.

Gold fell into the hands of your average citizen usually through the plundering of the Pharaohs tombs, as, much like the Mesopotamians, they were buried with vast hoards of gold. The most notable discovery in recent years of an ancient Egyptian tomb was that of the Pharaoh Tutankhamen, or "The Boy King". This was discovered by Howard Carter in 1922 and very nearly never became a reality. After many years of searching, Carter had failed to discover anything of significance. His quest was put on hold during World War 1 and resumed shortly after, yet still he found nothing. The expeditions were funded by a Lord Carnarvon, and after many years of wasted expeditions and expense, Lord Carnarvon offered him one final season out in Egypt and, lo and behold, Carter finally delivered one of the greatest discoveries of the century. Carnarvon travelled out for the exposure of the tomb, and when Carnarvon asked "Can you see anything?", Carter replied with the famous words: "Yes, wonderful things." As well as the Sarcophagus, the head of which most people in the western world will be able to recall from memory, there were also untold riches in gold and precious stones.

Today, Egyptologists estimate that 75% of the antiquities from the ancient Egyptian period are still buried. Treasure hunters from all over the globe still travel to Egypt in droves every year in the hope of discovering some of the riches still buried in the sands.

As we again advance from Egyptian times, different civilizations also started to adopt the use of precious metals as a trading medium. Every individual and society understands the intrinsic value of gold and silver, but not all revered it as the Egyptians did, as godlike substances. For a long time it still remained very much a symbol of status and was still only possessed by royalty and the wealthy elite. However, it started to trickle out of the hands of these people and into the hands of tradesmen and, from there, into the hands of everyone else. Granted, the average person would not have access to vast stores, but gold and silver were making their way from pocket to pocket, down the line until everyone was trading in gold and silver, no matter how minuscule the amounts actually were.

Following the Egyptians many years later, the Greeks and Romans brought huge advancements to the process of mining all types of metals, precious or otherwise. The Romans were the pioneers of a basic form of hydraulic mining, wherein they diverted streams of water to propel gold bearing sand over a sheep hide. As gold is very heavy, the hide would trap the pieces of gold no matter how small. Once this 'Golden Fleece' was saturated it would be dried and then beaten to recover the gold. The Romans in particular went back to many old mining sites with this and other technologies, and were successfully able to extract more gold from these mines. This primitive form of hydraulic mining was actually still being used by some miners as recently as the 1849 gold rush of California.

**The reason for this extensive mining and gathering of gold was primarily to be used in the further evolution of the manner in which we trade...**

# 4. Coinage

This system of trading in gold and silver worked very successfully for millennia, but was eventually refined even further during the ancient Greek era around 600 BC. They realised that having to weigh out these precious metals was time consuming and far from an exact science. What if the piece of gold you had to trade with weighed 1.4g, but you only wanted a loaf of bread at 1g. There is no chance anyone is going to give away more than they have to. Would you? That is nearly another half a loaf. Breaking up the gold piece to make it only 1 gram was trial and error and no easy task in itself, especially without the correct equipment to do so. So the idea to mint them into certified, standardized coins was created.

The very first coin on record was the 'Stater', brought into existence by the Greek colony of Lydia. The picture to the right is 1/6 of a Stater. This early coin really looks nothing like what we associate as a coin today. It is more of a nugget with a print on one side only. The material was not gold or silver, it was actually both. A naturally occurring amalgamation of gold and silver is known as electrum. The coin was made by placing a weight of electrum into a cast, and literally beating it by hand into the mould. As gold and silver, and so electrum, are soft metals; one side of the coin took the shape of the mould. The other would merely display evidence of it being beaten into shape.

The enormous success of the Stater for use in trade caused the concept of coins to expand rapidly. Coins were now being minted and used all over the ancient Greek civilizations. The Romans were surprisingly late adopters of Coins, and by the time they finally introduced their own coin the Greeks had been using them for over 300 Years. Another 300 years or so later in 27 BC when Augustus became the first Emperor of Rome, he became the very first person to have a likeness of himself printed on a coin. Many citizens, caring little for politics, would learn of a new Emperor when their face appeared on a coin. Augustus' rule was the first and longest out of all the Roman Emperors at 44 years, but due to some of the Emperors ruling for as little as only months, the very first act they usually performed was putting their face on coins.

As the Roman Empire aggressively expanded into one of the largest ever known and absorbed the Greek Empire, its influence over the world at the time was second to none. However, due to its sheer size, it became very difficult to govern, and in 285 AD the Roman Emperor Diocletian divided it in two, the Western Roman Empire and the Eastern Roman Empire, which would become known as the Byzantine Empire. After this point both east and west started to mint their own coins. There were a few Emperors who did still rule over both east and west, namely Constantine the Great who reigned from 306 AD - 337 AD, and who also introduced Christianity as the primary religion of both Empires. After the fall of the Western Roman Empire in 476 AD, the Byzantine Empire continued to refine the minting process until its fall just under a thousand years later in 1453 AD to the Ottomans. By this time their coinage was spread all over the globe. The minting process had been heavily refined, and both sides of their coins now held a print, one side displaying the current Emperor, the other with Christian iconography.

Let's apply coins to our fisherman, farmer and hunter; and say that each gold coin weighed 1 g. Very little changes, the loaf of bread is now 1 coin, a fish 2 coins and a side of venison 14 coins. No more messing around with dividing raw gold, you know that if you have 1 coin or 50 coins exactly what that buys you. The primary difference is the time taken to conduct transactions is a fraction of what it once was.

So now we have precious metals being minted into coins, and these coins had a set trading value, providing they are complete and the weight they are supposed to be. But, what if you removed part of the coin, even if in tiny, barely noticeable ways? The value of the coin has now changed! What if part of the coin were removed, but they were still being traded as the same value as when they were whole? This process is known as coin debasement, and there are two manners in which to do this.

The first is called sweating, in which coins are placed in a bag and shaken vigorously. As the soft metal of the coins collide with each other, part of them wears off leaving a residue in the bag. After sweating, the contents would then be painstakingly extracted from the material. This method of coin debasement was not very

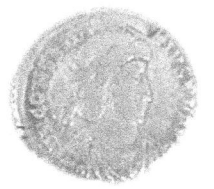

effective and extremely time consuming.  The yield was also low and hard to collect, but it did hold the benefit that it was very difficult to detect from normal wear and tear.


The second type of coin debasement is called coin clipping.  This is achieved by actually cutting part of the edge of a coin away, removing a slice or slither of the precious metal the coin is made from.  This can be seen by the coin on the left and the coin in the middle on the picture above.  Both are the same coin, just one has all it edges clipped.  As precious metals are soft and easy to manipulate this process was very easy, albeit highly illegal, and carried a maximum penalty of death if discovered.  To stop this happening, the artisans minting the coins introduced a reeding, or milling, to the edges of the coins.  As the process was further refined a text engraving was also added as well as the milling.  This can be easily seen on the pile of pound coins.  After this was introduced it would be very easy to determine if a coin has been tampered with.  Note the shape of the early coin as well, although spherical it is far from the perfect circles our coins are today.

Although we still use coins today, the shape and the use of a metal is where the similarity ends.  Early coins were mostly made of gold, silver or electrum, which in themselves hold value, whether in coin form or any other form.  The coins we use today hold value only because we are told they hold value, not because the base material they are made from is valuable.  In the grand scheme of things this is actually a very recent development.  Up until 1964, American coins were made of roughly 90% Silver, and it was not until the decimalization of British currency in 1971 that precious metals stopped being used in the minting process.

As with any solution, new challenges are created. With a standardized way in which to trade put in place, gold had now become one of, if not the most valuable commodity in the world because of what you could buy with it. This is very different compared to today, as even though gold is still one of the most valuable commodities, it is rarely used as a trading medium. Around 60% of the world's gold is used to create jewellery, about a quarter used for investment, and the remaining percentage is used in technology and for scientific research purposes. You wouldn't pay for something in a shop with your gold ring, would you? That is simply because it wouldn't be accepted. If you took a Gold ring worth £400 into a supermarket and tried to buy £50 worth of groceries there is not a chance that they would accept it as payment, even though the value of the ring is 8 times the value of the goods you are looking to acquire. The only chance you would have is if maybe an intelligent member of staff realised the potential value in the Gold, and offered to pay for your goods in exchange for the ring.

Again, this is a very recent development. Go back 50 years or so and the value of gold was appreciated considerably much more than it is today as a trading medium. Most of us just see gold as jewellery, nothing more. It might be something nice to wear that we know is valuable but we would never dream of trading with it except in extreme desperation. The remaining percentage see gold as a store of wealth and buy, sell, and keep gold as the market value fluctuates in order to make a profit.

**Trading in coins seemed like finally a solid and foolproof way to trade had emerged. So where exactly did this solution go wrong...**

## 5. Where it all went wrong

So how did this system of trading in gold coins and other precious metals come to spoil? As a trading system is was essentially perfect. A valuable material, cast in a set weight, that we pass between each other. But mankind is capable of doing amazing and terrible things, some of the worst of which are usually motivated by greed. Some people are just never satisfied and will always want more, usually for the power associated with wealth. Ever heard the saying "There is one golden rule, he who holds the gold makes the rules"? While correct, this can easily be taken much too seriously. The fear of loss is a powerful driving force that can make all but the strongest people compromise what they know is morally correct. What happens next is a prime example.

We now have this system where everyone is trading in minted gold coins. But how do you:

- Keep your money safe? The best chance you have is to bury it somewhere or attempt to hide it somewhere within your dwelling.
- Transport your wealth? The coins are weighty and carrying even a small amount of gold in a coin bag may draw attention, let alone transporting larger amounts that may require horse drawn carriages and even a bodyguard detail. This makes you are prime target for cut-throats and brigands.
- What about international trade? Thanks to the Romans, Europe has expanded and is now connected by road and sea. Can you imagine moving 10,000 gold coins from European mainland to England? Pirate ships are everywhere and always alert for precious cargo.

The answer was pretty straightforward really, and has been demonstrated a number of times already as a tale about a goldsmith. As it is such an effective way of spinning the tale of what happened next there is no need to reinvent the wheel.

So we have our goldsmith, who, alongside making jewellery and other goods with gold, is now in the business of minting coins. He owns a large vault in which to safely keep large stockpiles of precious metals used for his trade. Individuals and tradesmen who were making a good profit from their profession were easy targets for thieves, and for some people paying someone to physically safeguard their wealth may have meant the difference between making a profit or a loss. Finding such a person who would not just rob them further compounded the security issues for safeguarding wealth. Naturally, concerned about preserving their assets, the tradesmen decided to entrust their wealth to the goldsmith's vault, where they knew, or assumed, it would be safe. They paid a small premium on their deposits for this security, and in return they were presented with a piece of paper that could be used to withdraw their deposits when they required them. It was simple really. There is absolutely nothing wrong with this practice at all. It is no different at this stage from any other bartering transaction. The owner of the vault would allow others to use their service, and in return the depositors have to pay for the privilege of doing so.

What happened next was one of the biggest moves towards the currency we have today. Instead of people withdrawing their gold when they required it to make a purchase, people were actually trading the promise of the gold in the vault, against the goods they wanted to acquire. Put simply, the credit notes were being used in markets as the gold itself. These paper guarantees to the gold were lightweight and easy to transport., no great surprise really that this practice started becoming commonplace as it was much more convenient than going to the vault and carrying heavy coins around. It also came to light that other goldsmiths, even in other European countries, had experienced very similar occurrences. Eventually, even the goldsmiths were trading between each other for the promise of gold in each other's vaults. As acceptance and use grew and grew, this process contributed massively to further expansion all over Europe, as it reduced the need to physically move large amounts of gold from city to city, or even country to country. One could inconspicuously hide the promises of large sums of gold on their person, without raising any suspicion. In a time when pirates were rife, and cutthroats lurked down every alley, not drawing attention to yourself or what assets you may possess was a big deal!

Our goldsmith's job title is now changing, to start with he was much like any other smithy, refining metals into products. A blacksmith made horseshoes, armour, weapons and the like. A silversmith made jewellery and tableware. Our goldsmith also makes jewellery as well as decorative items, but he is now also running a business storing gold, as he is now renting out vault space to those willing to pay for it. All of these smithies would also have active trading relationships with many people to acquire the metals required for their trade. As the need for standardized sums of money was becoming widespread, our goldsmith technically was now a jeweller, vault owner and mint. A silversmith may also be experiencing something similar as silver coins were being minted as well as gold coins. It was only matter of time before his next bright idea.

"Why don't I start lending out my gold, for a price, naturally", and he did just this. So now the goldsmith had an income not only from gold the clients stored in his vault, but also from the increased return he demanded for his service of lending gold. The basic principle of this is how loans work today. We will loan you £20,000 over 5 years, but in return we want £28,000 for this service we are providing you. With the now widespread acceptance of the paper promises being traded freely and growing rapidly in popularity, people also started asking for their loans in the same paper promises instead of the gold itself, and why not with its widespread acceptance. It had become as accepted as the gold itself. In practice, as long as the goldsmith had enough money to lend there was nothing wrong with this at all.

So what is the main limiting factor of the amount of credit that can be given? Well, the amount of gold these goldsmiths owned personally you may think, and you would be correct. But when it was realised that hardly anyone came in to withdraw their gold, and people were asking for their loans in paper format as opposed to gold, the goldsmith started not only lending against their own gold, but also against his depositors' gold as well. This was of course highly illegal and punishable by death as most crimes were in that time, but in reality also very difficult to discover as only the goldsmith knew exactly how much was in his vault. As long as he kept a low profile and didn't raise suspicion there was no way he could be detected.

This seemed to work well, very well; for a time anyway. As long as all the credit given out was repaid, then there would be no issues. But, eventually, suspicion was raised due to the large quantities of credit that were being given out. Doubt set in, and depositors confronted the goldsmith, naturally concerned that their supposedly safe wealth was being manipulated behind their backs. Upon discovering that their deposits were still there, which they were, but loans were being made on their deposits, they wanted in on the action. What came out of this is that the goldsmith was no longer paid by depositors to keep their deposits safe, they actually came out with a small earning on their deposits, as long as the goldsmith could continue to lend against it. This is the principle of compound interest, and we are now moving closer and closer to how we bank today. From this point onwards the goldsmith has now turned into a banker, paying out a small dividend on gold stored, and lending it out at a higher interest rate.

During his tale of evolving from being a goldsmith to becoming a banker, there has been devious and deceitful tactics employed, but let's face it, it hasn't really turned out poorly for him. Even after being rumbled, the goldsmith has successfully managed to adapt to the challenges presented and to ensure his continued prosperity. After reading this, many of you will likely think that this is how banking works today, and to some extent it is.

**What happens next brings us much closer to modern banking and is where it becomes surreal...**

## 6. Insult to Injury

We now have our pioneer banker, so far detached from his original trade he can no longer be called a goldsmith. He has already worked through a great deal of illegal practice and adversity, but somehow has still managed to come out on top. His loans are now mainly given out in his paper format, and his depositors still rarely come to withdraw their gold, which was of course still safe in his vault. His next bright idea was the one which draws us to a little understood modern day banking practice, known as Fractional Reserve Banking. Even the title seems daunting and confusing, and rightly so, when you understand the absurdity of how it came to be.

Our banker, for all his prosperity, still wanted more, as is usually the case. After he has paid his depositors for the gold they are allowing him to lend, his percentage of the profit is now considerably less than before he was discovered. So what is his limiting factor here? Naturally, this is the amount of gold he has in his vault. So how can he increase his credit limit? He could increase the amount of gold he has, which would be the logical way to move forward. But that is not what he does. The contents of the vault are still known only to the Banker himself, and with this in mind he starts to create money for commocities he doesn't possess. He just makes it up out of thin air.

Yes, you read correctly! The banker conjured into existence credit against commodities he didn't even possess. The claim checks to the gold were now so widespread all over Europe that he no longer issued credit in gold at all, only his paper promises of the gold. This was by a good margin his most adventurous idea yet, but as hardly anyone ever came to physically withdraw their gold, the only way his plan could fail is if a substantial amount of people all came to withdraw their gold at the same time. In this case he would not be able to meet the demands of all his depositors. This is known as a "run on the bank", where there is physically not enough in a bank's vault to pay out.

For a time his plan worked perfectly, and nobody suspected what he was actually doing. Would you? Well, as good as his plan was he was indeed eventually discovered, and his worst nightmare became a reality. Word spread like wild fire, and suddenly after many years, even decades, of hardly anyone coming to withdraw their gold, everyone came at once. Game over! His most daring gamble yet had failed, and he had nowhere near the amount of gold he required to meet all the credit he had invented, and he soon ran out of gold.

What occurred next is just as absurd. His claim money was now so widespread that to render all of it essentially worthless would collapse the rapid expansion Europeans were now embarking on across the globe, as well as set back the progression of mankind by potentially centuries. It was the backbone of all trade, and provided the means by which we refined and invented new technology. We became more educated as a species, leading to new technologies like the printing press, cities expanded at a phenomenal rate, and the quality of shelter for even the poorest of families improved. In many ways it may have had its own part to play in the development of steam power and after that, electricity. In one hand the banker has actually done humanity a huge service, but on the other it was born from a hugely corrupt system that has hardly changed at all, even up to today. It may have brought great advances as an unintentional by-product, but the system itself is based upon nothing but pure greed and corruption, with no intention or consideration to anything other than furthering themselves.

So, as hard as it is to believe, the practice was actually legalized and regulated. Again the banker triumphs, even though his nefarious schemes have been exposed. It was agreed that the banker could continue to lend out more than he actually possessed, but must still adhere to a maximum amount of credit based on his deposits. This is how Fractional Reserve Banking came to be. The banks are now legally allowed to create credit out of thin air, and only need a small percentage, or fraction, of the credit physically in their possession.

To ensure that the bankers were conforming to these regulations, there were surprise audits. This was obviously a very prudent decision as the bankers have been making it up as they go along until now and clearly could not be trusted to be left to their own devices.

The value of this fraction varies from country to country even today, and is modified by each country as required so there is no global standard. Needless to say, as loans are borrowed and repaid, the amount of the fractional reserve increases, and so the amount of credit that can be given out also exponentially increases.

Let's say for instance that the fractional reserve ratio is 1:10. If an individual came to a bank for a loan of £10,000, all the bank would require is £1,000 to be able to grant that loan. When it was repaid in full, there is now £11,000 in the Banks reserve. The original £1,000, and the repaid £10,000. This £11,000 reserve would allow a loan or loans of up to £110,000. If this was all loaned out and repaid there would now be £121,000 in the reserve and would already allow loans in the £ Millions. Given the same formula with only a few further steps the amount is now in the billions.

This is also where central banks such as the Federal Reserve Bank, and the Bank of England came into existence. The smaller banks, now known as local banks, were connected to each other in a network, all leading back to a central bank. In the event that there was a run on a local bank and they were unable to meet withdrawal demands, these central banks would provide the local banks with an emergency top-up of gold. Even this was not fool proof, though. If enough people came to a wide enough spread of banks simultaneously to withdraw their deposits, then even the central banks would not be able to cope with the demand and the whole system would collapse.

Created in 1694, the Bank of England was the first ever prototype central bank, and created a model that every other country in the world would replicate. As throughout many periods in history, England was at war with France, and the credit of the government of William III was so poor that it couldn't borrow the £1.2 million it required for continuing the war effort, particularly rebuilding the British Navy. The Idea of the Bank of England was devised by the 1st Earl of Halifax Charles Montagu, and as well as having total control of the governments assets, it would also be the only establishment allowed to issue legal tender. Twelve days later the Bank of England had produced the funds needed to continue the War with King Louis XIV. In its infancy, the Bank of England did not possess the same power that central banks hold today, but it is undeniable that it paved the way. Over the following centuries, central banks would also be given the sole responsibility of regulating the value of a countries currency.

Another central bank worth noting is the US Federal Reserve Bank, created in 1913 with a view to maximise employment for the American people, prevent excessive inflation of the U.S. dollar, and provide a stable monetary system for years to come. Although there were many teething troubles and times where it seemed it had failed, ultimately it succeeded as it is still here today a century later. How much longer it will continue to function as intended is extremely questionable though.

The most important point to note with both these examples, the Bank of England and the Federal Reserve, is that they were both created as privately run institutions. The Federal Reserve is still privately run today, but the Bank of England, although privately run for most of its life, was nationalised post World War II.

**Now that Central Banks had country-wide control of wealth our perspectives of value had changed due to this paper money emerging. However, there is a difference between something that holds value, and something that does not...**

## 7. Money Vs Currency

At this point we have to detour slightly from our tale of the evolution of banks to clarify some terminology which will help us better understand the nature of the beast. We have now made a shift towards what the average person today calls money. But what we use on a daily basis isn't money at all, it is currency. Nearly everyone on the planet incorrectly calls currency, money.

Which one of these would you take if offered? There must be $10,000 on the left, and let's say, for arguments sake, that the gold is also currently valued at exactly $10,000. Keep your answer in your head as you read on.

Now take into consideration the following. Money is something that holds value in its own right. For something to be an effective form of money it must be:

- Portable - You have to be able to transport it easily. Livestock fail here as they are not easily transportable without great time, expense and hassle.
- Valuable - There must be a desire or a requirement for it. Certain shells were originally used as a form of money but these hold no value nowadays other than ornaments.
- Durable - If something is perishable it is not a good store of value. Food is a good example, although it holds value it is a poor store of wealth, as it spoils.

- Divisible - It must be able to conduct any transaction, no matter how small or large. Many commodities fail to be money due to this.
- Non-Consumable - A large amount of commodities are not money for this reason. Fossil fuels are a prime example as we actively use them up.
- Fungible - Must be easily interchangeable for something of a similar value. Precious stones are not fungible as they are difficult to exchange for something of a similar value.

Now take those gold coins above. They are easily portable, they most definitely hold value, metal is a durable material, they can be easily split, gold is hardly ever destroyed or consumed, simply reshaped, and finally it can be easily exchanged for something of a similar value.

The gold coins meet all the requirements of money. They are valuable not because we are told they hold value, but because the material they are made from is valuable. They are durable, easily exchanged and have their own intrinsic value in whatever format, coin or otherwise.

Now let's take a look at the dollars. Well they are portable for sure. They are NOT valuable in themselves, but hold value only as long as the currency is valuable since the paper they are printed on is worth next to nothing. Durable, well yes to an extent, but given a long enough time scale they will degrade, which is why old bank notes are eventually taken out of circulation and replaced. It is divisible with all the different denominations a currency has. With regards to being non-consumable it is questionable as we all know paper comes from tree's and we are slowly but surely exhausting our supply with deforestation; the dollars themselves are non-consumable but they are made from a finite resource.

Up until the last 40 - 50 years, dollars and pounds were much closer to money than they are today, as, if required, they could be taken to a bank and redeemed for their counterpart in gold or silver. The moment it was decreed that this was no longer allowed, notes could no longer be exchanged for precious metals, and coins were now minted out of base metals that hold very little value themselves. This is no longer money.

Currency is nothing more than a government approved form of legal tender, a medium of exchange declared fit for use by the powers that be. It holds no value other than that we are told that it holds value, and we are forced to use it as a replacement for money, but it isn't money!

When currencies collapse, historically, gold and silver always make a re-emergence, and they will be worth exponentially more than they are now. They will rise and rise in value until they meet or exceed the value of all currency within the economy. However, there is a big difference between what happened historically and today. Now we are all connected together through the internet, and not just person to person but country to country. The whole planet is inextricably linked together, Pound Sterling and American Dollars are not just in their home country. They are all over the world. Unlike previously, this time when the biggest currencies fail it will have ramifications on a worldwide scale like it never has before.

You don't have to be a genius or hold any special qualification in economics to detect that something big is coming, and has been for a good many years. The recent banking crises, the unrest in countries globally, rioting, and a worldwide sense of despondency are all signs of a larger event on the horizon.

**Which would you choose now?  The dollars or the gold?  Still have not made up your mind?   You probably will after the next section...**

## 8. Fiat Currency

As we all well know, the banks are now not just controlling Europe, but are dominant all over the world. The primary difference between our goldsmith turned banker and today's system is that there is actually no longer any gold or commodity reserves behind the banks, all these figures and countless billions are entirely fictitious. That is not to say that the banks no longer own precious metals, because they do, just that what we now use as money is no longer backed by these commodities as it used to be. We actually trade each other in lies and promises for commodities that no

longer exist at all. What we trade in now as fiat currency is actually debt, not value. The word fiat is not in reference to the Italian car manufacturer, but is derived from the Latin, where it means "An authoritative order, or official decree". This can be easily confirmed when you take a look at the how the wording has changed on paper money/currency over the years.

This early dollar bill clearly states: *One Silver Dollar, Payable to the bearer on demand*. If required, this could be exchanged for its counterpart in silver at a bank. It is a claim check to a commodity.

Can you see the same anywhere on this Dollar bill? Not at all, it is merely telling you: ***This note is legal tender for all debts, public and private.*** This is now a fiat currency, not money.

The American Dollar was last reformed during the presidency of Richard 'Tricky Dick' Nixon, who in 1971 stopped allowing the conversion of dollars to gold and silver. This is when it stopped being money and became a fiat currency. These new dollar bills cannot be redeemed for their counterpart in silver, and the silver is more than likely not even there anymore. Since the creation of the Federal Reserve in 1913 the US Dollar has lost more than 95% of its value. Just over 100 years and it is worth a fraction of what it once was due to becoming a fiat currency.

Fiat currency is simply something which has been declared by a government as legal tender, but holds no intrinsic value, just an exchange of debt between our fellow man. Yes, you can buy goods and services with it, but that is only because we are forced to by our governments. Hard to believe that when you buy your latest smart phone, or do your shopping at the supermarket, you are handing over the claim to someone else's debt that has been invented in the first place.

The first sparks of fiat currency actually go back a lot further than Europe and that is where our goldsmith turned banker story continues. The Song Dynasty of China during 10th century AD was historically the first to issue a paper currency called Jiaozi, but it was plagued with issues and as a result was short lived. Centuries later, the next Dynasty, the Yuan Dynasty, improved on the mistakes of the Jiaozi, and was much more successful in introducing a paper method of trading, known as the Chao. However, due to the Mongol warmongering and the subsequent inflation that goes hand in hand with wartime, the next dynasty, the Ming dynasty, scrapped the paper currency and went back to copper coins.

*"All these pieces of paper are issued with as much solemnity and authority as if they were of pure gold or silver...and indeed everybody takes them readily, for wheresoever a person may go throughout the Great Kahn's dominions he shall find these pieces of paper current, and shall be able to transact all sales and purchases of goods by means of them just as well as if they were coins of pure gold".* - Marco Polo

Throughout history, fiat currency tells a very definite tale. None of them last! Out of the many thousands of fiat currencies that have ever existed, the average life is only 27 years. The shortest lifespan of a fiat currency is a single month. The only fiat currency that seems indomitable is the British Pound, founded in 1694, making it 320 years old to date, and still going strong today. That being said, much like the dollar of 1913, £1 used to be made of 12oz of silver; if this were still the case each coin would be a massive investment in its own right. As it stands today compared to the price of silver, and being made of a base metal, £1 is less than even single percent of its original worth. What is clear, though, is that eventually every fiat currency becomes worthless and even the seemingly immortal British Pound will not live forever.

Contrary to popular belief that the governments account for most of the fiat currency created, their piece of the pie is actually tiny compared to the amount invented out of debt by the banks. The ratio could be as much as 95% created by banks from debt, and only 5% created by governments, but the two are still inextricably linked. Governments provide the banks with a fiat currency through which to give out credit. They also enforce that debts be paid upon default of a payment, including collection of collateral should the debt fail to be paid. But the single most deceitful thing governments do is pass laws to ensure the banking system prospers and is kept in good standing with the public; mainly by making it all so obscure that most citizens can't understand it or just don't want to know. All this information has been on the internet for years, if not decades, yet the mainstream media has provided virtually no exposure on any of it.

Another little known fact is that the vast majority of fiat currency is now digital anyway. If you think that all the currency in circulation exists somewhere as paper notes or metal coins you could not be more wrong. As much as 90% of all fiat currency is now digital, just being saved in the banks hardware and passed from account to account without anything physical ever being produced. There have been various reports which are ever increasing in frequency that shops and even major companies are refusing to take cash as payment for transactions. What do they know that we don't? One of the most notable examples was a disabled woman in America who waited outside an Apple store to buy their latest iPad technology with 600 bucks ready in her purse. Upon reaching the head of the queue she was told "we don't accept cash", or words to that effect. It even clearly states on the notes that it is legal tender for "ALL" debts, public and private. Yet it clearly isn't if you can be refused a transaction. This is not limited to technology giants though. There are further cases of retail shops in every industry now refusing to accept legal tender such as coffee shops or computer stores; an example could probably be found for any industry in America.

As established very early on, if faith in a currency is lost then there is no longer any desire to obtain it since you cannot use it in future transactions. Over the coming decades it would be a solid prediction to say that all physical fiat currency will be taken out of circulation and we will only have debit and credit cards with which to conduct all trade.

**Still want those paper dollars now?...**

# 9. Icing on the Cake

Now we tie all that we have learnt so far and apply it to modern day banking practices. The process is very similar to fractional reserve banking, only now we know that the fractional gold and silver reserves aren't required to exist anymore. Instead of a commodity functioning as the fractional reserve, fiat currency is now the fractional reserve. So something which has been invented in the first place is a reserve for more to be fabricated into life.

Every time a new loan or mortgage is approved, or even when governments borrow off the world's private bankers, new currency is simply typed into a computer and, hey presto, there it is...magical debt, issued in a currency that has no lasting value and written into the borrowers account.

The main problem our modern day banking poses is that, as debt is being created in the form of fiat currency each and every time someone borrows, it can never be paid back. The banks are creating debt and then charging interest, creating further debt that can only be paid back by....creating more debt. It's an endless cycle! We are all in the pocket of the banks. Individuals, businesses, corporations and even governments all borrow off the world's private banks. With our current system we actually rely on a state of perpetual debt. This state of perpetual debt requires constant expansion of our economies just to keep up with repayments.

A utopian society wouldn't be one that is constantly expanding as is defined by the monetary system of the world's private banks, it would be one that is constant and stable. If we managed to reach the ideal where a country could produce all its own energy from green sources, not have to borrow at interest and so constantly be forced to expand its manufacture, agriculture and infrastructure, it would grow and grow until it reached the point where it was sustainable and then stop. When it reached that stable point there would be no further need for growth until the population boomed. Unfortunately, this is simply not possible with the monopoly the world's banks have and the control they exert on each and every one of us, keeping us perpetually in their pockets. They are literally leaching and amassing the entire planets wealth.

When countries are in recession, individuals, companies and governments find it increasingly difficult, or even impossible to repay the interest. When this happens, whatever was placed as collateral against the loan is absorbed by the banks. Practically every asset on the planet is now owned by the banks in some form or another, physically or on paper as collateral.

In 2009, when quantitative easing, or QE, was introduced, mind numbing volumes of currency were injected into the American economy. Hundreds of billions of dollars were created out of nothing by the Federal Reserve and given to the banks, who paid themselves record bonuses for crashing the world economy...wait what?

The truth of the matter is that if no one ever requested credit in the form of loans and mortgages, then there would be nothing to lend, as it is created during this process. As the amount of credit that can be given is limited only by the amount of debt, there is technically no ceiling to the amount that can be fabricated. When the bankers stop lending money, the amount of a fiat currency dwindles. This has been seen over the last 5 years with all the worldwide banking crises, causing economies to implode globally. The irony is that during these times the banks actually lend less money, stunting the economy further.

In long term loans such as mortgages and government borrowing, the initial or principle sum can actually be less than the interest. That's right, the extra money owed through borrowing actually surpasses the original amount granted. This simply cannot be paid so more debt must be created to pay the original debt and so on and so forth in a never ending cycle where debt will never stop increasing and new fiat currency will not stop being brought into existence.

So why do we do it? Well as long as we allow it to happen we really have very little choice, our governments impose fiat currency as legal tender and we have to use it. As mentioned previously with the gold ring, try walking into a supermarket and paying for your shopping in gold. The gold may be many times the value of your shopping, but there is no chance that it will be accepted. This is due to a misconception that has been driven home to us our entire lives that fiat currency is what we should be trading with and not money.

But what if our governments didn't borrow money off private bankers and took it into their own hands. If this was the case our tax money would go a lot further into improving the economies of our countries, better transportation, renewable energy, agriculture and manufacture. The majority of what we pay in income taxes is actually to repay the interest our governments have incurred by borrowing from private banks. That is not someone else's wealth. That is you as a taxpayer paying off the debt that has been created when your country borrows off private banks. There has been a great deal of evidence to suggest that income tax would only be a tiny percentage of what we earn should this practice not be allowed. There would still be council taxes for the upkeep of your local infrastructure, but what is directly deducted from your earnings would be a fraction of what it currently is.

So why do governments allow this practice?  Surely a country can produce all the legal tender it needs itself without having to borrow from the worlds private banks, at interest.  Well it has been attempted before, by great men with vision who saw just how wrong the banking system is, but none have yet succeeded.

*"Whoever controls the volume of money in our country is absolute master of all industry and commerce, and when you realise that the entire system is very easily controlled, one way or another, by a few powerful men at the top, you will not have to be told how periods of inflation and depression originate". -* James A Garfield, assassinated President of the USA

*"The government should create, issue, and circulate all the currency and credits needed to satisfy the spending power of the government and the buying power of consumers.  By the adoption of these principles, the taxpayers will be saved immense sums of interest.  The privilege of creating and issuing money is not only the supreme prerogative of the government, but it is the government's greatest creative opportunity".-* Abraham Lincoln, assassinated President of the USA

Whether pauper or president, no individual is safe.  Anyone who challenges this system of absolute control is simply erased.  People argue who is the greatest superpower. Is it the US, China, Russia?  The answer is none of the above.  It is the banks.  It's a scary prospect, one that makes most people put up and shut up even when they fully understand it.  But these private banks are run by a miniscule amount of the planet.  Let's say there are 10,000 of these private Bankers.  10,000 against over 7 billion people on the planet is an extremely small percentage. If we all one day just said we will no longer tolerate it, the whole system would come crashing down. It only prospers as long as we use it.

*"Beneath this mask there is more than flesh. Beneath this mask there is an idea, Mr Creedy, and ideas are bulletproof."* - V For Vendetta

While individuals are easily controlled, imagine if an entire country rebelled against the monetary system. There is strength in numbers and, as a collective, mankind is unstoppable, something that many of us often forget as we live in our own little bubbles. Many of us now live in what has been described as a "Cocoon Society". Our houses are our forts and our temples. Decades ago everyone would most likely know who their neighbours were; it is quite common, if not standard, nowadays to never have even spoken to your neighbours. We have receded into our own places to escape and let everything go on around us, but that is not the answer. Progress and change never happened by running from the problem. It is the product of confronting the issue head on and having the strength of character to follow through on what you believe, no matter how much adversity you face.

**"None are more enslaved than those who falsely believe they are free".** - Goethe

**Not only do the banks keep us in perpetual debt, they have another tool in their arsenal that they can use to meet their ends. Though it does not always work in their favour...**

## 10. Inflation & Hyperinflation

With the fiat currency we have today the main problem is that, as and when governments or central banks want to print more currency, they can. At a whim, more credit or debt can just be brought into existence out of thin air. But this is not without consequence. When more currency is created, it also drives down the value of said currency. This is the reason why precious metals will always hold value. There is a finite amount of them. Yes, the price fluctuates, sometimes wildly, but they will never lose their worth.

If there was twice as much gold on the planet would gold still be as expensive? Not at all, you would expect it to drop by half in price. If there was only a tenth of the amount of iron, would it remain so cheap? The principle is the same.

If a country is not extremely careful about how it injects fiat currency into its economy it can have disastrous effects. However, when correctly employed, it can be turned to advantage. If you suddenly inject a huge amount into an economy, the value of the currency will fall per unit and prices will skyrocket, this is known as inflation. A common misconception is that the price of goods increases but this is not the case at all. What is actually happening is, as the value per unit is being driven down, you will need more of that fiat currency to purchase your goods and services. Basically, as more currency is injected into an economy, your purchasing power is being driven down. This is how inflation can be used alongside interest to further exert control. However, sometimes it doesn't go as intended, or, more worryingly, maybe it is all preconceived.

When large amounts of currency are injected into an economy, and it is combined with a loss of faith in the currency and/or other economic issues, this is known as hyperinflation. Prices escalate out of control as the currency becomes less and less valuable per unit, and people stop caring about using their national currency or keeping any savings in that currency, the complete opposite of the desired effect. These times are again when gold and silver make a re-emergence, that reliable fall back that we go back to again and again. Good old barter also comes to the surface again. Hyperinflation and war alone account for 41% of all failed fiat currencies. Sometimes, this may be the desired effect, as when you crash one currency there is an opportunity to create another. These times are also when revolution occurs so it is a very risky game to play.

The most notable example of hyperinflation is of the Weimar Republic in Germany post World War 1. In 1923 Germany failed to meet a repayment and compounded with great financial hardship for every citizen following the war, experienced hyperinflation on an epic scale. Much like the recent quantitative easing, Germany flooded its economy with marks. To add to that, there were strikes all over the country in all industries and very little was being produced as a consequence. Over an 11 month period from January 1923 to November 1923 the price of a loaf of bread had gone up from 250 marks to 200,000,000,000 marks. Many people will have heard the story of Germans turning up with wheelbarrows of marks for a single loaf of bread. Wages were handed out in suitcases and there were even reports of the suitcases being stolen, but emptied first. What was actually valuable there was the case, not the billions of marks inside. Some people even sold their houses to survive the crises, and weeks later the currency they had would afford only one loaf of bread.

Hyperinflation, as wrong as it sounds, is also an enormous opportunity for those positioned correctly. One individual borrowed enough to buy a large herd of cattle as the crisis was starting and shortly after paid it back in full by selling a single cow. Property will change hands many times during these times, usually out of the hands of hardworking people of the country and into the hands of a minority with enormous wealth and no morals. Once things stabilize again they could find themselves owning entire towns or even large areas of cities, which will then most likely be rented back to the people they were taken from.

So why during the last 5 years has America not been experiencing hyperinflation when they have injected billions of dollars into their economy? This is due to a process so obscure and devious, but one that will ultimately come back to haunt them, with unimaginable consequences. America has been 'exporting their inflation'. So how exactly does that work? Quite simple really, as all these new dollars are injected they are using them to purchase products and services from overseas, shipping their dollars out of the country. The result of which is that all these extra dollars are not floating around in their own economy and devaluing it or significantly increasing the cost of their products.

But this is what the Americans might say is only a 'Band-Aid'. Yes it is offering a temporary solution, but what happens when faith in the dollar is destroyed? Suddenly, all these dollars that are spread around the world come flooding back and, when that time comes, something hits the proverbial fan. The resulting hyperinflation could potentially be the worst ever recorded. This story could potentially make the hyperinflation of the Weimar Republic look like child's play.

However, it is not just the US who has been injecting enormous volumes into its economy. Every country on the planet has been expanding its fiat currency since the banking crises, each one having at least doubled, in many cases tripled its supply of fiat currency in circulation since 2008. It took America 200 years up to the financial meltdown to reach $825 billion as their total amount of currency in circulation. On Christmas day 2013 there was $1.24 Trillion in circulation as stated by the Federal Reserve website. That is $415 billion fabricated in the last 6 years alone, just greater than 50% of what it took 200 years to reach.

Ultimately, the main issue with inflation is that the people who are actually driving our economies are the ones that suffer. The buying power is being taken out of the hands of the farmers, the factories, the educational system and other essential infrastructure, and doing nothing more than lining the pockets of the world's private bankers as they sit on their pedestals grinning inanely at how gullible we all are.

We now have in excess of 7 billion people populating our planet. Are you aware that over 2 billion of those, around 30%, live on less than $2 a day! Many people in economically developed countries wouldn't get out of bed for $2. During Quantitative Easing 2, or QE2, the knock-on effect was that global food prices increased on average by 60%.  Can you imagine the effect that had on the people already attempting to live on a mere pittance.  Our basic survival needs again come into play.  If we really wanted to, even today, we can seek shelter ourselves for free outside the concrete jungles, even a cave would serve.  Granted, compared to what we now accept as the norm in our nice warm houses it wouldn't seem like much, but it would serve to shield you from the elements.  One could find fresh running water at no cost from springs in the countryside.  Where we really struggle nowadays is nutrition.  We have long since evolved beyond being hunter/gatherers, and unless you are a farmer by trade most of us only know how to buy food.  Some may have private allotments to grow their own vegetables, but this is still a small percentage of the population.

Can you imagine working 40+ hours a week and at the end of it food is so expensive there is nothing left over.  What about the people who work 70+ hours a week and face that exact problem.  Inflation's effect on food prices is the most dangerous threat to the banking system, food scarcity has been at the heart of nearly every, if not every, single revolution in some capacity.

**"They say that every society is only three meals away from revolution. Deprive a culture of food for three meals, and you'll have an anarchy."** - While this quote is most famously from cult TV program Red Dwarf, Robert Grant and Douglas Naylor were not the original authors, it remains a point of speculation as to who the original author was.  Whoever the author, this message is very profound.

**With all this bound to come to a critical point soon how do you protect you, your loved ones and your assets?  What can you do to ensure that the fiat currency that you have, no matter how**

much or how little, will be worth something tomorrow?  In short,
how do you store wealth safely?...

## 11. Old School Wealth Protection

How do you ensure your survival and even comfort through times of financial uncertainty? Very simple really, while the existing system is in place we are forced to use fiat currency to acquire the goods we need to survive, and pay our bills and our rent. But what happens when that currency collapses? You could have £10 or £10,000,000 in your bank account, but this is all now worthless. It is nothing more than digital numbers and printed paper that mean absolutely nothing. What you need to do to ensure your survival or even prosperity through turbulent or revolutionary times is store your wealth as money and commodity, not currency. Something that holds value no matter what the economic situation. Hopefully after reading this far you will know how to do that, but here it is one more time, gold and silver!

As a country's currency collapses we once again revert back to before our goldsmith story started. We will once again barter with each other. A farmer will have wealth in livestock and crops, and will have real buying power. Anyone in any kind of production trade, particularly food, will prosper as they will never find someone who doesn't need what they have on offer. But right at the top, precious metals like gold and silver will reassert

themselves as they always do.

Start shifting your wealth out of fiat currency and into something that actually has value.  Keep as much as you need to survive in fiat currency and anything left over use to safeguard yourself for the times ahead.  The price of gold and silver at this moment in time is extremely low, namely because there is more on paper than in existence.  There has never been a better time to start investing!

So you may be asking yourself, should I buy gold or silver?  The answer is both.  They each hold their own different qualities.

Gold we all know as being the ultimate commodity since it is very valuable and in a time where many of us have known nothing other than fiat currency it seems like the immediate option.  Every one of us understands that gold is one of the most sought after commodities, and because of this preconception it will most likely remain the most sought after commodity in our minds eye.

Silver is a sly one though, and often gets overlooked.  It would not be possible to publish or even write this book without it.  Silver is a core requirement in so much of our technology due to its electrical and thermal conductivity being second to none, compounded with the annual demand for silver being much greater than the amounts we are mining each year.  When the time comes, silver will increase rapidly in value compared to gold.  Yes the value of gold will increase massively, but silver will increase at a much higher rate by comparison.  This is because it is actually consumed, whereas most of the gold that is available today is either in jewellery or being used for investment.


How do you buy gold and silver?  Nowadays, there are some great websites to do this from.  Firstly, you would decide if you want it physically in your possession.  If yes, websites like bullionbypost.co.uk are ideal.  This would be a good option for people wanting to buy and store. Simply pay the current fiat price and they ship it to your doorstep. You can buy in coin or bullion, and in many denominations from 1g to the 12.5kg bars we associate with gold vaults. It is actually very easy to hide a fair value of gold in some obscure location within your property. Half a kilogram of gold is currently around £13,000 at time of publication, this is about the same size as a normal chocolate bar.

Another option is to have it held in trust. This means you don't physically possess the gold and silver, but you can own some that is stored in a vault. While this manner may seem easier, you will be charged a small percentage for storage. This method is best for people who want to trade rather than just sit on some precious metals. If you aren't trading and are just doing it for investment, the value will slowly depreciate as storage charges are taken off. Using websites like bullionvault.com you can purchase and sell gold and silver very easily. Stripping it down to basics you buy in troughs when the price is low, and sell when it peaks, or rather

 **BullionVault**
Safest Gold, Lowest Prices

"If there's an easier route to buying gold I have not found it"

when it reaches a value you are happy selling at. The biggest mistake any person can make when trading is getting greedy, sitting and waiting for it to reach a previous peak and having the bottom fall out before it reaches that value and actually making a significant loss. That being said, when done correctly it can net you a tidy revenue stream.

One must always proceed with caution when purchasing any commodity though. Do some research first! Is it a good time to buy? What is the market currently doing? These can make a difference between making a profit and throwing away your wealth. There are many websites where you can track the price of gold &silver. What is it doing in the last week? The last month? How does this compare to the last year or even 5 years? Another point to note is that you are essentially gambling. Okay, your odds are a lot better than in a casino as you are making educated decisions based on fact, but there will always be forces outside your control affecting the market. Stick to a simple rule of thumb. If you can't afford to lose it, don't invest it!

**People have been storing their wealth in this manner for thousands of years, but in 2009 everything changed...**

## 12. BitCoins & Crypto-Currency 101

Now we are onto the real meat and two veg! In 2009, a revolutionary new manner in which to trade with each other and store our wealth was born. The BitCoin. What exactly is BitCoin you may be asking yourself? BitCoin, or BTC as they are often abbreviated, is a type of crypto-currency. What is a crypto-currency? Put simply it is a peer to peer (P2P) way of transferring funds from one individual to another, anonymously, and without involving any type of financial institution. As it is not controlled by any country or central bank, this has created a decentralized "Money of the People", putting you once again in complete control of your own assets.

BitCoins were brought into existence by a mysterious programmer known only as Satoshi Nakamoto, which is the Japanese equivalent of John Smith. Satoshi Nakamoto is widely thought to be a pseudonym for a collective of programmers, none of which have ever given an interview.

A great deal of mystery surrounds the creator, or creators, of BitCoins.

BitCoins can be broken down to 8 decimal places, or 100 Million pieces. Therefore, 0.00000001 BTC, known as a Satoshi after its creator, is the smallest denomination possible. As they are easily divisible into many parts this checks one of the boxes that makes them an ideal form of Money. Let's look again at the requirements for a successful form of Money:

- Portable - BitCoins can be sent online very easily from one person to another across the BlockChain, where transactions are handled.
- Valuable - They are valuable as they offer us something unique, a way to store our wealth outside the banks, and charging fractions of the costs for international transactions.
- Durable - It is more durable than gold and silver, it is totally non-perishable as you cannot maliciously destroy its code, though you have to be careful where you store them.
- Divisible - A BitCoin can be split down into 100 million pieces and can be used to conduct any transaction large or small.
- Non-Consumable - BitCoins are never consumed, just handed from one person to the next, they are never used up.
- Fungible - BitCoins can be exchanged for anything of a like value providing that they accept BitCoins.

As we can see here, BitCoin is just as successful a form of money as gold and silver, potentially even more so as they are much easier to store. The codes from your BitCoins can actually be taken off the internet and printed onto a piece of paper. Compare $10,000 of BTC to storing $10,000 of gold or silver. The BTC codes would fit in your wallet and you wouldn't even feel the weight difference of the piece of paper, try carrying that much precious metal on your person; you would feel it weighing down your wallet or purse. They are also easier to divide as you can send exactly how much you need.

For the first couple years of its existence, BitCoin remained pretty much unknown to anyone other than computer enthusiasts, particularly users of the TOR browser. TOR stands for 'The Onion Router', and is a modified version of Firefox that allows you to access deeper parts of the internet inaccessible to normal Firefox, Google Chrome, Internet Explorer, or any other standard browsers. In TOR, your traffic is sent through a proxy where it will be routed through potentially hundreds of IP addresses, making it very difficult but not impossible to trace. Though it is not commonly known there are actually "Levels" on the internet, and what we access in our standard browsers on levels 0, 1 and 2 is only a tiny amount, as little as 10% or less. Level 0 is called the 'Common Web' and consists of the vast majority of websites we visit on a day to day basis. Level 1 is the 'Surface Web' where sites like Reddit appear. Finally level 2, or 'Bergie Web', is where sites such 4Chan are found. The rest is hidden from the average user on Levels 3 and above or below, whichever way you look at it; and require you use TOR browser or other means to access it. Here is where the internet gets insane as you progress into the 'Deep Web'. Here you can find all kinds of things, amazing and terrifying. Every time you penetrate deeper and deeper into the internet you uncover more and more that will blow your mind or simply revolt you. It is only recommended for the very strongest of mental constitution, and only accessible to IT geniuses whose brains must work in binary.

Gradually though, over the years since 2009, BitCoin gained the attention of the media and public. Since 2011, interest has rapidly increased, most notably during the enormous rise in value of BitCoins in April 2013. In 2011 a single BitCoin was worth only $0.30, in 2013 a single BitCoin has been worth in excess of $1250 at its peak.

As a type of digital currency that is based on cryptography for security, it is impossible to counterfeit with current day technologies. When technology advances into quantum computing there may be a potential threat to the security of this cryptography, but that is many years from becoming a reality; and by then, quantum cryptography or something similar will be put in place to ensure continuing security. The American NSA is supposedly just starting work on a quantum computer and has received many millions of Dollars to fund their research, but it is only that, research. Chances are quantum computing will take billions to make a reality and research will be painstakingly slow. A quantum computer would be capable of processing unimaginable amounts of data simultaneously, and no encryption we currently know would be safe from a quantum computer. Much like malware that is written today though, adequate protection will be put in place when the time comes. Whenever a new virus is created our anti-virus software discovers it and protects your computer from it. The principle is exactly the same.

There are a finite number of BitCoins in the world, with a hard-cap of just under 21 Million set to be reached by 2140. They are created as a reward for mining "Blocks". The coin value of a block is 50 BitCoins for the first 210,000 blocks, 25 BitCoins for the next 210,000 blocks, then 12.5 BitCoins, 6.25 BitCoins, and halving on and on with each 210,000 mined; until in 2140 there will be no more blocks to mine. As there is a hard-cap on the maximum amount of BitCoins, there no possible way for a central bank to issue a flood of new BitCoins; which would lead to devaluation of those already in circulation. In this sense, BitCoins are much closer to a commodity like gold and silver than they are to a currency as we understand it. Technically they are crypto-money, but we so widely use the word currency now in the wrong context that it is hard to escape this misconception.

Apart from mining, BitCoins can be bought and sold in return for fiat currencies on several exchanges. They can also be directly transferred very easily across the internet from one user to another. More on mining and where to buy and sell in subsequent sections.

You can also directly spend your BitCoins for products and services

on any websites that accept it. Initially only a handful of sites accepted BTC, however the range of products and services is expanding at an alarming rate. In the decades to come it is very likely that BitCoins will be accepted everywhere as a form of legal tender, albeit not in the conventional sense as fiat currencies are. As anyone can send BitCoins to anyone else in the world and it avoids fiat currency exchange rate fluctuations and additional processing charges banks impose sending currency to other countries.

The pioneer, and powerhouse of crypto-currencies is the BitCoin, however there are now many others, some of which like LiteCoin (or LTC) have also established a strong foothold. There are new crypto-currencies appearing all the time, though many of them seem ill conceived when compared to the big players. Some coins have billions or even trillions as their hard-cap, immediately driving down the market value each coin is floating at, simply because there are just so many of them. Just like BitCoin, they are mined through presenting your computer's hardware with challenges for it to solve.

There is a great deal of speculation regarding Crypto-Currencies, some are calling them a bubble, pyramid, or a Ponzi Scheme; though it is no more any of these than any other form of fiat currency. Less so in fact! Others are embracing it fully and looking eagerly forward to the future where BitCoin and/or other crypto-currencies make all fiat currencies obsolete. When you compile all the evidence about how we manage wealth currently and understand just how broken the system is, feeding our buying power into the hands of the few; one can only hope that for the prosperity and advancement of mankind that this will become a reality sooner rather than later!

**Hopefully you have a rough idea of what exactly Crypto-Currencies and BitCoins are now. Now for some more detail...**

## 13. BitCoin Storage

If you are interested in acquiring BitCoins, but have no prior knowledge, then this is as good a place as any to start. BitCoins are very flexible in the manner in which they can be stored, although some options are more secure than others. The most important thing to note at this point about storage is that ultimately you are in control over where they are stored, and how secure they are. There is no central bank controlling them, and very few financial regulations controlling them...yet. As a result, if you misplace your BitCoins, or have them stolen then they are gone. Not only are they gone but no authority will care about it either. If you went to the police and said you had BitCoins stolen, most of them would be clueless, and, as there are no regulations for them to follow, it will simply be dismissed.

While this may sound like a negative point, safely storing your BitCoins isn't actually that hard to do. So what are your options?

**1. Store them locally.** Local storage refers to keeping them on your computer. BitCoins are stored in what is known as an eWallet. You can download the BitCoin client from the following website https://bitcoin.org/en/download. Once installed it may take a considerable amount of time to synch up with the network as it will have to download every block mined since BitCoins were launched back in 2009. Even with a fibre optic internet connection and a powerful PC this could take in excess of a whole day. The interface is very simple to use, if you navigate to the 'Receive' tab it will show you your eWallet addresses. You may change your payment address as often as you like, or use as many as you wish to. This sequence of numbers and letters is what you use to receive payments in BitCoin, likewise on the send tab you can input addresses to make payments to. If you settle for this method of storage it is recommended that you immediately put a very secure password on the client. This can be done by clicking 'Settings', then 'Encrypt Wallet'. Do not use any password you have used before, and make it extremely complicated using upper case, lowercase, numbers and special characters, and ensure it is of a decent length. NEVER store this on your computer; it's like leaving a safe unattended with the key next to it if someone did manage to penetrate your computers defences. Write it down and keep it in a safe place. If you are storing your BitCoins on your own computer, it is highly recommended that you also have an adequate security solution. This is your first line of defence and is the same as anything PC related; ensure you have a strong anti-virus program, firewall, and malware and spyware cleaner. If this is a grey area to you then the following programs are recommended. Avast Anti-Virus Free version is a very good program that doesn't interfere much with your system as other anti-virus programs can. Windows basic firewall is usually more than adequate for the job, however if you wish to upgrade your firewall then Comodo provides an excellent free version, it can be a little inconvenient with pop-ups but that is the price for security. It will inform you anytime a new connection is made to your computer, or when something tries to modify a system file. With regards to malware and spyware, Malwarebytes Anti Malware, commonly referred to as MBAM, is one of, if not the best out there. This program checks for things that anti-virus software generally doesn't pick up, spyware, key loggers and the like. Running this once a week is very beneficial.

**2. Store them Online.** There are now a great many websites where you can store BitCoins, but exercise caution as to the reputation of these companies, and how good you think their security solutions are. Some websites are just eWallet, others are eWallets built into exchanges where you can convert your BitCoins into fiat currency and vice versa. Some of the most secure places to keep your BitCoins online are on the major exchanges; Bit Stamp, BTC-e and BTC China are the three biggest in terms of volume and reputation. Up until very recently MT Gox was also one of the big players, but they have become insolvent after all their BitCoins, and anyone who stored BitCoins with them, were subject to a highly sophisticated attack which stole 750,000 BTC. Do not let this deter you from using online eWallets however, as the majority are reputable and secure. Once you have settled on an exchange or online eWallet, simply create an account with them with an ultra-secure password and log into their service. Once logged in it functions exactly like the local BitCoin eWallet. In your accounts page there will be your address to receive payment, and a place to send BitCoins to others if you have their address. Major exchanges are probably the most popular method of storing BitCoins as they can also be bought and sold, as well as converted into fiat currency with ease. More on this later.

**3. Cold Storage.** Ironically, as a digital currency, it is actually possible to print off your BitCoins. There are a number of companies offering a service to do this. An example of which is safepaperwallet.com which used to offer a kit that you could purchase, now the software is totally free. The benefits of printed Bit Coins are fair ly ob vio us

66

in that you are not trusting the security of your coins to a 3rd party, or having to worry about anyone penetrating your computer security. You can just print them off and keep them in a safe, or any other secure location.

**4. BitCoin Vaults.** These are relatively new concepts wherein you entrust your BitCoins to a vault where they are also stored cold, on a computer not connected to the internet. Apart from safe storage, while your coins are with these companies they are also insured, which is the only service of its type to currently offer any level of cover for BitCoins. As with anything, though, this service comes at a price. From the few companies that are currently offering these services, a 2% annual charge seems to be the standard.

**Coming up next, how to populate your eWallet with BitCoins...**

## 14. Mining BTC

Where do you acquire BitCoins to fill your eWallet? Well, as mentioned in the previous section, they can be obtained in two manners, mining, or buying. This section will look at the mining process of BitCoins and what purpose it serves.

As established, BitCoins are mined in blocks. What is a block? How do you mine a block? Let's take a single BitCoin. This BitCoin will have been mined in a block with other BitCoins, and has been produced as a reward for mining that Block. Mining what block you may be thinking? It gets a little technical from this point in, but hopefully by the end of this section you will have an understanding of how it all works.

The mining process has two primary functions. Firstly, it generates new BitCoins as reward for whoever mined that block. Secondly, it is the method in which BitCoin transactions are authorised. Remember that the BitCoin network is peer to peer(P2P), and there is no single establishment like a bank that checks and authorises transactions, anyone currently connected to the mining network is validating the transactions for everyone. If it helps, think of a block as an A4 sheet of paper with a to-do list on it. When someone works through this to-do list, they are checking the validity of the transactions on it, and the manner in which it does so means it is impossible to double spend. Once someone has completed this to-do list, they are paid a reward in BitCoins.

If you wanted to send a BitCoin to your best friend, the people who are currently mining BitCoins are authorising that transaction for you. This process is immensely sophisticated and complicated but put very, very simply, it checks you have the funds available in your eWallet and, if you do, it moves it to whichever eWallet address was specified. Every block is strung together in what is called the BlockChain. This is publicly visible and every transaction ID, or TrxID, can be looked up which will detail which address it came from, which address it went to, and the amount authorised. How is this anonymous? Well, you never have to enter your personal details, ever. Although every transaction that ever took place can be looked up, it will never be tied to you personally.

So, how do you mine? Even today this is still an area little understood by many, mainly because it requires a very high level of proficiency with computers. This section is not designed to give you a step-by-step guide as to how to set-up mining, just explain the process. Once you have set-up the BitCoin client on your computer it will have generated you an address to receive all BitCoin payments. You will then download some mining software, point it at your address and set it going. Although that sounds like the most simple thing ever conceived, an understanding of computer command prompts is required to use many mining programs. There are some with nice GUI's (Graphical User Interfaces) that are easier to navigate, but these still require a high level of computer proficiency to make them work.

A common occurrence for miners is to form what is known as a 'mining pool', where a network of computers all contribute to the mining effort. When a block is mined you will be rewarded with BitCoins proportionate to the effort your system provided to the pool. If someone solves a block you are working on before you then it will be rejected as stale, and you get nothing. By being part of a pool you significantly increase your chances of finding and solving a block, though you then split the reward between those mining it based on the power you contribute. Although you get less per block than solo mining, being part of a pool allows you to find and solve more blocks in the same time when compared to solo mining. All in all the return is fairly similar to solo mining, just that mining in a pool will be more a lot more consistent. While solo mining you may not solve a block for months or even longer, but, when you do, you get the full reward. Mining in a pool gives you a constant fraction of coins mined.

The issue for the average home user mining BitCoins is that the greater the power contributed to mining a block, the difficulty increases proportionately. There will only ever be a set amount of BitCoins generated each day, but if there are 10,000 people mining, it is easier to solve a block than if there are 1,000,000 people mining. Originally, BitCoins could be mined from a home system using its processor (CPU). Nowadays there are potentially many millions of people mining BitCoins at any given time, compounded with the fact that there is dedicated hardware available whose sole purpose is to mine BitCoins. These are known as ASIC rigs, and they serve no other purpose than to contribute to the mining network. An important term to learn here is 'Hashing'. Hashing power basically equates to the amount of work you can perform, and how much you are contributing to the mining process. The greater your hashing power, the more you are contributing to the mining network, and so the greater the reward in BitCoins.

Let's take a CPU that may have been common during the early days of BitCoins, an Intel i5 2500K. This CPU should put out around 20 MH/s, or 20 Mega Hash's per second. The ASIC hardware at the time let's say does 100 GH/s, or Giga Hash's per second. Hopefully you see where this is going. Based on those numbers the ASIC hardware outperforms the home CPU by 5000 times, and is the sole reason why BitCoin mining is now very difficult for the home user to hop on board and see a return.

The newest ASIC cards are now performing into Terra Hash's per Second (TH/s). If you are unclear at this point about what these words mean, each time it goes from Mega to Giga to Terra it is a multiple of 1000. 1 MH/s = 0.001 GH/s = 0.000001 TH/s. Let's say that a new ASIC card is performing at 1 TH/s, this single piece of hardware is now performing the equivalent of 50,000 home computers mining on an Intel i5 2500K. If the 50,000 home users and the 1 individual mining on their ASIC hardware were mining the same block, with no one else contributing at all, then out of the current 25 BitCoin per Block reward, 12.5 BitCoins would go to the 1 person mining on their ASIC hardware, and the remaining 12.5 BitCoins would be split between 50,000 people; granting them a mere 0.00025 BTC each. You may be thinking that it isn't a fair comparison taking a 3 year old CPU and comparing it to a modern ASIC card. However, although CPU's have obviously increased in processing power, in terms of Hashing Power though, when compared to ASIC advances, the difference is negligible. Even if the latest Intel CPU's put out 100 MH/s that would mean there would be 10,000 people not 50,000 to equate to the 1Th/s ASIC card. That is still 12.5 BTC to the individual with their ASIC set-up, and the remaining 12.5 split between 10,000. This still only equates to 0.00125 BTC to each of the 10,000.Another crucial point to make here is that these ASIC rigs run on a fraction of the power that a home PC does, comfortably below 100 watts. Someone mining on their home PC would probably struggle to break even against the power cost nowadays mining BitCoin, as a half decent home PC would demand at least 300-400 watts under full load; potentially much higher than this for a very high spec computer.

So why isn't everyone mining on ASIC hardware? It is ludicrously expensive that's why. A single current ASIC card putting out 2 TH/s could cost you in excess of £5,000 per card, they can also be stacked next to each other, and that's exactly what some people do. There are BitCoin mining 'farms' worth £millions. The other reason is that although most of the companies selling this hardware will say it will pay for itself in 'X' days, this remains a highly debated area on the internet. The companies advertising their product are basing their figures on the current difficulty of mining BitCoins, if another 10,000 people started mining BitCoins, each with 2 TH/s of power, the difficulty would rise considerably, meaning your reward per block would significantly diminish. Not only that but 3 months later another company brings out a 10 TH/s model for the same price, and everyone buys those; further diminishing your return. The people who are really profiting from mining on ASIC hardware were the first people to buy in, when it was brand new technology and no one else was using them. The first ASIC miners would have made such huge profits from BitCoins that it is probably still keeping them going and buying the latest tech out of their initial profit even today.

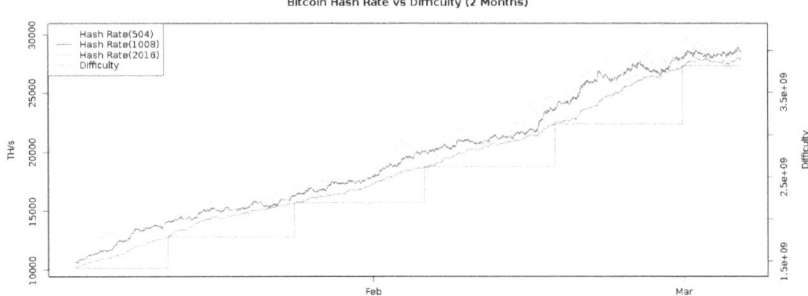

Bitcoin Hash Rate vs Difficulty (2 Months)

As can be seen in the graph above, the hashing power has taken since the release of BitCoin in 2009 to January 2014 to reach 10,000 TH/s, and in the last 2 months alone the Hashing Power has tripled and is now 30,000. There are many people who will also argue that ASIC mining is totally financially viable and will provide a return on investment. They have maybe experienced this themselves. While this is not intended to deter anyone at all from purchasing ASIC hardware, at least there is a potential flip-side for people to consider before parting with their hard earned cash. BitCoin mining is only viable nowadays using ASIC technology. That is an absolute. If you want to mine BTC then this is the only way to go. If you decide you are going to invest in some of this hardware make sure when you are calculating your potential profit that you take into consideration the change of difficulty over time. There is clearly a market for mining BitCoins and the companies selling ASIC cards are obviously doing very well as they are constantly releasing new models with greater hashing power. If any of this section sounds negative it is not supposed to be, but one needs both sides of the story before making an informed decision.

**If you don't think mining BitCoins is for you then how else can you obtain them?...**

## 15. Investing & Trading BitCoins

Now you hopefully understand a little more about BitCoins, the mining process, where you keep them, and the transaction process. You may decide that mining is not for you, but realise it's an enormous market that is growing each and every day. How else do you get a piece of the action?

You may wish to just invest in BitCoins long term to buy when the price is low, or even just buy them in the hope that they will reach some of the targets estimated. There have been predictions that BitCoins could hit anywhere between $10,00 to $100,000 in 2014. Others have predicted that eventually BitCoins could total the entire supply of fiat currency for the whole planet, putting each BTC at over $1,000,000 each. These are by no means guarantees, just an educated opinion, but needless to say many people are looking at BitCoins as a long term investment. Buy now and sit on them for years in the hope they skyrocket again like they did in 2013. If this sounds like you, then you will want to know where you buy.

There are two primary methods to buy BitCoins, OTC (over the counter) websites such as bitbargain.co.uk and exchanges, like btc-e.com.

OTC websites are buying and selling between users, just like you. It is free to create an account and start using these services, though a transaction fee will be deducted for the seller. This is a very simple way of obtaining BitCoins, though you may not always be getting the best deal.

The second is to use the major exchanges, BTC-e, Bit Stamp & BTC China. These websites are considerably more functional than the OTC websites and include graphs and other data that can help you make an informed decision regarding when to buy and sell. If you are considering trading BitCoins then this is the way to go. BitCoin is still a very volatile market, and extremely susceptible to high profile events affecting the price. At the end of 2013 when China halted all BitCoin transactions the price dropped significantly. More recently, with the collapse of one of the biggest exchanges, Mt Gox, the price of a BitCoin again bottomed out in what has probably been its most significant drop since its meteoric rise in 2013. However, to a trader, this is far from a bad thing. A highly fluctuating market means there is an enormous potential profit to be had, if one buys and sells at the correct times. Some days BitCoin has differed as much as $150 between its peaks and troughs, while still maintaining the same average price. If you had 1 BTC and bought in 5 troughs for the day at say $500, and sold each time you bought in at $650 peaks, that is $150 profit per trade, 5 times = $450 out of a single coin in a day. Imagine if that was 10 BTC, or if you executed 10 trades, or executed 10 trades with 10 BTC. Now it really isn't as simple as that or everyone would be doing it, but the potential is definitely there to make a large return if done correctly. In reality you may buy in one day at what you thought was a low price, and the bottom falls out again, meaning you have actually made a loss for the day. You may have to sit on those BitCoins for another day, a week, or even longer before it rises again to where you bought at. This principle is no different to how fiat currency is traded against each other on the Forex. The right trade, bought at the right time, and sold at the right time can make a fortune.

There are also other tools at ones disposal to aid in the trading process. The graphs on the exchanges, while functional, usually don't have a great amount of detail. They show you the trend, but not the fine details. Websites like bitcointicker.co are invaluable when trading as they have a huge amount of detail on their graphs, as well as being able to switch them between the different exchanges as they all trade at slightly different prices.

If you want to get serious about trading BitCoins then another weapon in your arsenal is the mainstream media, and dedicated BitCoin news sites. If something makes national, or even global news with regards to BitCoin then that should give you a strong indication as to whether the price will be due to rise or fall. If a country announced that BitCoin is now accepted as legal tender, the price of BitCoin would rise as confidence in using it as a trading medium has risen. Contrariwise, if a country announces that it is banning trade and use of BitCoin, then the price would fall. There are pointers everywhere to keep your eye out for.

Another manner, besides OTC and Exchanges you may or may not have heard of are BitCoin ATM's, that function much like normal ATM's, but let you convert Fiat Currency to BitCoin. The world's first was released in Vancouver, Canada in November 2013, though they are now spread across the globe, with more popping up all the time. These offer a very simple way to buy BitCoins, though they far from widespread enough yet to be a primary manner by which to buy.

**BitCoin is not the only Crypto-Currency out there, what about the others?...**

## 16. Algorithm's & AltCoins

A term you may have heard if you have already had exposure to BitCoins and other crypto-currencies is AltCoins. If not then no matter, all will be explained.

An AltCoin is any crypto-coin that isn't BitCoin. Following the birth of BitCoin since 2009, other crypto-coins were created that used the same technology utilized to make BitCoin work. The cryptography BitCoin utilises is called SHA-256. There are other crypto-coins based of this algorithm as well, the most notable being NameCoin (NMC) and PeerCoin (PPC), all working on the SHA-256 cryptography. Some are carbon copies of BitCoin with a different name, others have their own little niches as they attempt to overthrow the BitCoin and become the No.1 Coin; but, as of yet, none have succeeded.

In October 2011 the first coin that doesn't use the SHA-256 Cryptography was released, the LiteCoin. LiteCoin uses SCrypt as its cryptography rather than SHA-256. But without understanding the technology in finite detail they are just words, with one major difference you need to know about. SCrypt Coins, with their differing cryptography, cannot currently be mined using ASIC devices. There are ASIC devices currently being developed for SCrypt coins at the time of publication, but these are not set to be released until the summer of 2014. What does this mean to you? Well, it means that all SCrypt Coins, of which there are now hundreds, can still be mined using powerful home computers. Anyone can still have a go at mining SCrypt Coins.

SCrypt Coins, although they can be mined using a CPU, are mined most efficiently by using a computers GPU (Graphical Processing Unit); specifically AMD graphics cards. There are two competitors for your money when purchasing a graphics card, Nvidia, and AMD (previously ATI but were bought out by AMD in recent years). They are both built differently internally, and while for general top end gaming or rendering performance, Nvidia has been at the top of the food chain for some years now, the AMD architecture outperforms Nvidia's for mining SCrypt coins many times over. As a result of AMD's superior SCrypt mining performance, the sale of top end AMD Graphics cards has gone through the roof.

If you were put off BitCoin mining due to the high barrier to entry with the ASIC devices, but wanted to give mining a go then, mining SCrypt coins is the way to go; for now at least. Much like the BitCoin mining process, you download mining software, point it at

your eWallet if you are solo mining, or at your pool if you are part of one and set it going. There are various pools available that actually automatically switch between the AltCoins mined based on how profitable they currently are. Mining LiteCoin is still possible from home computers as well, but more often than not there is a more profitable SCrypt coin to be mining. Setting up on one of these multi coin pools may take some time initially as you may end up with 20 different crypto-coins and need somewhere to send them all. The biggest exchange that currently handles every crypto-currency out there is cryptsy.com. Here you can turn any crypto-currency into any other crypto-currency very easily. You can even set a sell order at a target price and when the AltCoins reaches that value it will sell for you. Again, a bit of lateral thinking is required, and disregard any greed you have as it will ultimately be your downfall.

Are there any other types of cryptography? Indeed there are, there is SHA-3 cryptography known as Keccak. Recently Max Keiser, who has, in terms of numbers, been the most listened to individual on crypto-currencies, released his own coin on the SHA-3 cryptography. While this had the potential to be a serious threat to BitCoin, the launch was a riddled with issues and, because of this, faith in the coin was destroyed. Crypto-coins are no different than fiat currency in this sense, there has to be a faith in the currency for it to hold value. Very few managed to successfully mine MaxCoin when it was released and so it pretty much flopped before it even had a chance to get started.

Also worth noting is the PrimeCoin, abbreviated to XPM. The mining process of this coin not only authorises transactions and produces a Coin as a reward for mining, it also uses the Hashing Power to calculate chains of Prime Numbers, which in themselves hold value; and so add value to the Coin itself. To date it is the first to use Hashing Power to solve mathematical objects as well as the usual mining results, but it will not be the last. Cryptography that utilises its basis on real world objects as well as the usual mining result is something that is likely to gain momentum in its development, especially if there was a dividend paid out on such coins if and when these objects are sold by its developers. Instead of just wanting to obtain coins to trade into Fiat or BitCoins, if a dividend was paid out when objects were sold then there would be a reason to keep said coins, increasing their fiat value potentially many times over.

Finally, if you want to get started mining AltCoins, then there are numerous websites out there where you can track the current difficulty and profitability of all these AltCoins. Websites such as coinwarz.com. While their list is by no means complete, if you are wishing to mine specific AltCoins then sites such as this are invaluable reference points to aid you in your decision as to which coin to mine. You can even input your current hashing power, enter your energy costs and it will calculate how long it will take to mine the equivalent of a BitCoin based on the Hashing Power at your disposal.

**So where has this journey taken you?...**

## 17. The Great Unknown

Like so many things, a crystal ball would be more than just useful. All you do can is follow the signs and act upon them when you feel the time is right. Nobody truly knows where we will be in the next 10 years, 5 years or even next year; but if you look hard enough there is some very definite evidence developing. As a wise man once said...

**"The more distant we look into the past, the farther we can see in to the future."** - Winston Churchill

Based on the evidence of how Fiat Currencies all eventually become worthless, the average life being just 27 years, and how commodities always make a re-emergence when they fail; it would be a fairly logical prediction that something enormous is due to happen to the world economy soon.

There is no doubt that digital currencies are here to stay, with more and more legislation being released and drafted every day, but their journey is just beginning. BitCoin will most likely be around for many years to come, however it may not always remain the market leader. There is a view expressed that, much like the film Highlander, there can be only one. Currently that is unequivocally BitCoin, and it is likely to remain there for the immediate future. However, there is nothing to say that another, even more practical and efficient crypto-currency may knock BitCoin off its pedestal as crypto-currencies evolve.

So what exactly can you take away from all of this? Knowledge is power, and if you don't want to get left behind then arm yourself appropriately. Hopefully you will now have a good base knowledge to expand upon, and when asked about BitCoins and crypto-currencies, can stand up and be counted as not being totally in the dark. You will also have gained some insight into various manners in which to store wealth. If you now feel like dabbling with some trading just remember one key point, never put all your eggs in one basket, and never play with what you can't afford to lose.

Best of luck in all your endeavours!

VibeNode

This book will also shortly be available as a Kindle book and also as an audio book.

The audio book will be available as a download from www.webstersaudio.com and also from www.russellwebster.net

Also available through Snafu publishing are a wide range of informative self-help/personal development books and audio books.  These can be found both on Amazon -

http://www.amazon.com/mn/search/?encoding=UTF8?&field-keywords=russell+webster+snafu

or type in to Amazon  Russell Webster Snafu

The audio books will also be available as a download from www.webstersaudio.com and also from www.russellwebster.net

Finally, may we recommend SNAFU the book-available from Amazon.

It is a most unusual psychology, self-help book that is written with a  storyline.

Contact us - russell@snafu.co

www.ingramcontent.com/pod-product-compliance
Lightning Source LLC
Chambersburg PA
CBHW070300290526
45791CB00003B/1022